Already Everything

A Little Book on Seeking and Liberation

Copyright © 2020 Neil Denham

All rights reserved.

No part of this book may be reproduced in any form or by any electronic or mechanical means, including information storage and retrieval systems, without written permission from the author.

ISBN: 9798651780723

Cover Photo: Copyright Andy Hiam

There is no enlightenment,

Liberation never happens,

There is no-one who needs to awaken,

There is no-one who can awaken,

Liberation is the end of the need for liberation,

This is already everything...

Contents:

Non-duality	9
No-thing and Everything	11
L'apelle du Vide	14
Once Upon a Time	21
The Hokey Cokey	26
Innocence and Wonder	36
Words on Thoughts	41
Words on Teachings	47
A Little Visit to the Cinema	52
A Glimpse in the Matrix	56
Words on Neurosis	62
Words on Love	67
The Glass is Always Empty	74
Smoke and Mirrors	79
Resonance and Resonating	84
Timelessness	88
I Dream of Buddha	92
The Lake of Nirvana	96
Nothing Happening	101
There is an Epilogue (But it isn't Special)	105

Non-duality (Not two)

How can one describe non-duality?

It is impossible because non-duality is beyond all description.

In a way, non-duality, is too simple and too obvious to describe, because it is already everything. It is already the "absolute" appearing as "this".

Non-duality is not an acquired "state" or realisation. Neither is it a teaching which can be studied, learned, or understood, because the essence of that which is "non-dual" is unknowing.

When speaking or writing about "non-duality" subjectively, it is purely conceptual. It is an attempt to point to a mystery, which is, of course, entirely futile.

So, in that sense, everything that is said about "non-duality" is not non-duality.

Which means everything that follows is just a story…

No-thing and Everything

This is all there is… there isn't anything else.

This is already everything that "is" and "isn't", which is unknowable.

It is what appears and what apparently does not.

"This" is the great mystery, the "infinite" without limitation, without potential, and without any intention to be anything at all.

Everything is not a thing. It isn't even a really, *really* big thing. Therefore, everything is no-thing. "This", is no-thing and everything appearing as whatever is arising.

Within "this", there can also arise an experience that this is not everything, and that something needs to happen for "this" to become its totality.

There can be a sense that something has been lost, is missing, lacking, or that there is still something yet to be discovered.

This is the culmination of an experience that we could call separation, a feeling of being apart from the whole. This experience arises with the knowing of *"I am"*. This knowing *is* separation.

Because separation feels uncomfortable or unnatural for the individual, the response to this experience is to begin to look for something which is thought will bring about a sense of unicity.

That is why you think you are here, reading this book, or attending non-duality meetings. This book, and non-duality meetings, are simply a response to that seeking energy.

This is a natural responding to the appearance of that which becomes identified with as *"me"*, and an exposing of that appearance as being entirely unreal.

This is "no-thing" here, meeting and responding to an apparent "something" there, which is also no-thing. So, in that sense, there is absolutely nothing to be gained for the seeker or the responder.

"This", which is no-thing being everything, can never be found because there is no-one looking for it. It is already *"this"*, exactly as it is, which is perfectly and naturally whole.

There is nothing that needs to be discovered, and there is nothing that needs to happen, because "this" is already complete. There is no separation. "I am" is a dream. A lucid dream from which no-one ever awakens.

Sometimes this is heard or recognised, and that which experiences itself as being separate, can suddenly dissolve back into the whole…

L'appelle Du Vide

As far back as I can remember, I was always baffled, frightened, and intrigued by the human experience. There were so many games afoot in the game of life, I could barely keep track. All the intricacies and fragilities of being a person and having to share this life with other apparent people, seemed to get more and more confusing as time went on.

I was, as most people are, adaptable enough to get by, and over the years I adopted certain strategies for living that worked well enough for the most part. But the increasingly overwhelming sense was that I had somehow become well and truly lost, without ever having gone anywhere or done anything.

The response to this sense of being lost was a feeling that I had to find my way again. Although a child with a broad imagination, I never imagined for a moment that this feeling was in fact the calling to come home.

At a very early stage in life, human beings seem to acquire and then grow up with a fundamental sense of a something lost or missing. Some are more sensitive to this than others, but one could say that every human endeavour is a response to this sense of loss and the consequent longing for home.

Despite my own efforts and various endeavours, home was never found. The search to find this unknown "something", that was imagined would bring about the fulfilment I longed for, seemed always to be just beyond my grasp.

There was also, ultimately, a realisation that what was being looked for was not to be found in further education, money, a fruitful career, sex, drugs, meaningful relationships, or a plant-based diet. The problem isn't that everything just mentioned didn't bring about a sense of fulfilment, some of them absolutely did... for a while… it's just that the need for something more always seemed to re-present itself.

For me, the solution to this apparent dilemma was to start looking for something deeper and more meaningful, and so began my many endeavours into the seeking of something more "spiritual" in nature. There are, of course, as many definitions for what something "spiritual in nature" is, as there are people who would describe themselves as being "spiritual", or on a "spiritual path".

Personally, I would take on whatever path or teaching that seemed most appealing at the time; Zen Masters and their koans, martial arts, spiritualist churches, self-styled gurus, Christian mysticism, Hare Krishna, poetry written by Taoist immortals, quantum healing, re-aligning my energy centres, cleansing my aura, spiritual discussion groups, meditation retreats, holistic medicines, full moon drum circles, or more simply, the self-help section in my local library or book shop. But there was never an arrival point, there was only ever a *"what's next?"*

Although many of the subjects explored were no doubt helpful in their way, in that they may have temporarily appeased the psychology here, *(except for the drum circles, that's just insane)*, the tendency was to eventually get bored and rubbish whatever it was I had been exploring, because this next thing I had heard about was going to be the thing! *(What that thing was I couldn't possibly say? ... I never found out in the end).*

Then I heard about something called non-duality, which seemed to be trending at the time. There was a myriad of non-duality "teachers" available on the internet. There seemed to be a "non-dual" solution for every kind of problem. However, there was something most unusual about a small few who were describing non-duality and awakening in a way that made no sense to the mind whatsoever but was somehow recognised immediately.

I had inadvertently discovered a handful of speakers who were sharing something that absolutely pulled the rug out from under my feet. Everything that was being described ran contrary to all my dearly held belief systems and spiritual discoveries… Yet it was *absolutely undeniable*. It also seemed to pull down the pants of many of the popular speakers on self-help and spirituality of the time. This very much appealed to the anarchist in me, which I had never managed to outgrow, despite my efforts!

There was now a kind of instinctive aversion that arose whenever I heard an enlightened teacher or guru giving advice or instruction from the levity of their podium or metaphorical hilltop, no matter how apparently humble their confessions and servitudes.

I had been introduced to a new and radical concept, which was that all my endeavours to bring about awakening were quite possibly sustaining the very thing that was appearing to keep it hidden… Me. Which, with a little more clarity, eventually became, *all my efforts to find meaning, purpose, and personal fulfilment, were completely, utterly, and devastatingly hopeless… Because there isn't a "Me"!?*

As I continued to listen, all the gooey, dreamy ideas of what enlightenment should or would be like were swept away by the energetic tidal wave of what was being shared. It seemed to begin with an unravelling of the misunderstandings and false ideas surrounding awakening and liberation, until nearly all the spiritual "woo" was gone. *(I was always secretly a little worried about being a beautiful snowflake of awareness. Although a charming notion, it seemed to carry a lot of responsibility).* So, in a way, this came as a strangely welcome relief.

However, what was being said was more than a little disconcerting at the best of times, because of its uncompromising and confronting nature, not to mention its utter ungraspable-ness. Yet, as the call of the void beckoned once more, the irrational urge to jump was ultimately irresistible.

Just this nothing which is the extraordinary ordinary,

A marvel without meaning and purpose, time, or space,

Everything, everywhere, nowhere, no centres, no edges,

An apparent dying into empty fullness, raw, alive, and indescribable,

Just this absolute-ness which is and is not,

This is home for no-one.

Once Upon A Time…

Once upon a time, there was a sudden and profound recognition of the obviousness that is "what is". It seemed to manifest as an unexpectedly deep relaxation of the contracted sense of "self". A lightness became apparent in the body, and somehow in everything else. There seemed to be an un-desensitising. Everything started to get louder and louder, and it wouldn't stop.

For some weeks, it was as though the "self" would disappear or hide, sometimes seemingly for days. What was left during these periods was an overwhelming, if not more than a little unnerving, "empty spaciousness". The emptiness in everything was almost unbearable, but also strangely wondrous. All that appeared seemed almost entirely unreal... fragile... tenuous... insubstantial... as if it were somehow suspended with nothing behind it to hold it in place.

Then the mind would manage to re-assert itself and start to spin with a thousand questions and a heart breaking need to know what was happening. This was a very confusing period. Sometimes it was outright torturous, as though the mind and body were being energetically waterboarded.

There was a calling of some of the speakers that were being followed on the internet for answers or reassurance of some kind. Although all that were spoken with were very receptive to the call, kind, and generous with their time, there was never an answer or the reassurance that was hoped for. It all seemed so desperately hopeless and very unfair!

Then, quite suddenly, it was all over. There was an "I" pouring coffee from a pot one morning, and then there wasn't. The energetic sense or knowing of "here", just simply dissolved... *Whoosh!* ...Gone.

(It is impossible to realise or become aware of the contracted "me" energy whilst it is still being held in the body. It goes entirely unnoticed until the tension dissolves or falls away. It is an all-pervasive tension, which appears to be in everything and everywhere... until it isn't.)

There was only "this", which is "what's happening"; "empty fullness", "timeless being", "space-less spaciousness", "everything and no-thing", it was all the words that I had heard used in the describing of "what is", and it was none of them.

What was also startlingly apparent is there isn't, and never was, a "self", that can or could fall away. The whole experience of "I am" is a dream of something as really happening, but, in the natural reality, is not. That which seemed to have been, suddenly, never was.

All need to know or to understand also collapsed. As did meaning and purpose. There was just obviousness. So much so, that this was recognised as being very simple and totally ordinary, *"Almost not worth mentioning",* as was once heard said.

There was no angelic light descending from the heavens or emanating from within. There was no knee trembling experience to speak of. There wasn't even a stopping of what was being done. What followed was simply a sitting down and drinking coffee, for no-one.

What is, is just another story about something called "What is".

"This" is never spoken of, heard, or experienced,

There is nothing to gain, nowhere to go, and nothing to realise,

"This" is never understood.

The Hokey-Cokey

Nothing really changes in liberation. No-one really drops away, as there was never a "someone" there to begin with. Nothing needs to fall away or collapse for wholeness to become whole.

Then again, nothing is the same…

There is no longer an experience of life as being lived. There is just life naturally happening. There is no more grasping for or wrestling with whatever arises because there is no-one left trying to make it fit into a story called "me". This is the end of the story and there is no epilogue.

There is no real sense of cause and effect, so there is no real sense of the passing of time. There is apparent cause and effect, and apparent time, but there isn't an experience of one thing moving into the next. There is just immediacy… Just "this". Very simply, and very ordinarily, just what appears to be happening.

Also, because "this" is infinitely free and whole, there is nothing that needs to happen, and nothing that needs to be sought after or found. Therefore, all sense of meaning and purpose collapses, along with any and all notion of there being an "individual person" or "ghost in the machine", with free will, who is making choices and decisions in order to navigate from A to B or here to there. There is just what arises. Meaning, purpose, free will, and choice, serve only the illusory seeker still trapped within the dream of itself and is trying to find its way out.

In many ways, after the appearance of "me" disappears, there is more left than one might think. "Neil" the character, seems to continue. If anything, in liberation the character is now entirely free to be the natural character because there is no agenda to satisfy, and no roles to play. I don't imagine that friends, family, or colleagues would even notice a difference. It's not as though there is a coming out of the non-dual closet. There is no "Mum, Dad, I think you better sit down…" conversation to be had.

There are still many of the old familiar preferences and tendencies, such as a preference for Italian coffee, or Earl Grey tea, and a tendency to drink it in a favourite mug. A preference to arrive early for something, but a tendency to run a bit late, to name but a few.

I think it's fair to say that in liberation, many, if not all, efforts at self-improvement drop away. Certainly, the driving of oneself to seek personal fulfilment is over because there is no more person and there is nothing to fulfil. There is nothing needed in that sense.

Some hobbies and interests seem to remain, although you couldn't really call them "hobbies and interests" in the personal sense, they are just what happen. There is no story around any activity which may or may not arise. There may be a natural interest or curiosity in something, or an energy that wants to pick up a guitar and play for a while.

Jobs and careers may or may not change. It could be that getting up early every morning to go and work fifty hours a week at a stressful job will eventually become too bothersome? Who can say? However, it is unlikely that a job would just be dropped if there are bills to pay and no other means to do so, although it is not unthinkable.

What seems just as likely, is that there could be an accepting of a promotion with more money and more hours. Or maybe there will be more of a preference for spending time with family and friends, so there will be a switching to a job with less hours and less money? Who can say? There are no rules to freedom.

There may be more of an inclination to stay at home and watch television? Or there may be joining an evening yoga class? Whatever happens is just what happens. There is no-one in the driving seat or at the centre of strategic operations anymore. There is no more throttling the life out of life just to have an experience of more life. Life, or aliveness, is already what's happening. There cannot be more of what is already.

Maybe a strong wish to travel and see the world will arise? Or perhaps, any desire to visit other places will disappear entirely, because the garden is "really quite nice this time of year"? There is no-one who needs to go anywhere or do anything, because there *is* no-one, and everything is already being done.

This is just an attempt to point to the openness and freedom of it all. Life seems to continue, but without the meta-physical straight jacket. There is still an apparent responding to situations and events as they arise, but without there being any sense of a person here doing it. It's instant *"this!"* as it arises, and *"this!"* appearing to respond. There is no need whatsoever for there to be an additional "me" energy hanging around and making a muddle of things. This is the stunningly simple and natural way of it.

There is still an enjoying of spending time with friends and family. If anything, there is more of a natural enjoyment as there is no social positioning going on anymore. There is also no need to please anyone, or impress upon anyone, so there tends to be a natural relaxation, for the most part. It can be that there is a response to the energy of certain characters or situations which may manifest as dislike and these characters and situations are avoided.

There may have been all kinds of so-called bad habits prior to liberation and there may still be bad habits afterwards. They may even get worse for a while as "me" seems to employ all kinds of strategies to manage behaviours it thinks are objectionable in its attempt to safeguard itself in its story, or at least it thinks it does.

Having said that, when there is a leaving for work in the morning it is highly probable that there will be a wearing of clothes. A being conscientious still happens, as does self-care and personal hygiene, apparently… *(Except for sometimes on a Sunday or Bank Holiday)*.

It just simply does not matter what happens, if it happens, or when it happens. There is no-one left, so there is nothing relatable being experienced in the personal sense anymore. This is not a kind of acceptance or a becoming detached, when there is no longer a "me" at the centre of what is happening, there is no longer a happening to accept or detach from… Who would be accepting or detaching? Happenings only happen for "me". Without "me" there is just "this". Things of any real importance are only relative to the story of "me". When the story ends, so does anything of any real importance.

Something does seem to occur that recognises the necessity of setting an alarm if there is a preference to be up early enough to miss the rush hour traffic. If the car is running low on petrol a mental post-it note usually appears with "*Don't forget to stop for petrol*", and if it is forgotten there is usually a sudden energetic newsflash with the headline, "*You didn't get petrol!*", at which point there may be an utterance or two whilst looking for the car keys to go out again.

The brain and nervous system appear to continue to do what is necessary to ensure the survival of the body. There is the wearing of a seat belt when driving and there does not seem to be a tendency to drive down the wrong side of the road. If there was a being "jumped" by a man with a knife, there would be a running away. There is still a natural regard for one's safety.

(I once read a comment left below a YouTube video of an interview with a well-known radical non-duality speaker which said, "If all of these non-dualists say that there is nothing happening and everything is just an appearance, why don't they go tight-rope walking across a canyon and then see what happens?".
Well, that's because one doesn't typically become an idiot or a psychopath with liberation… As far as I know?).

Sometimes this message can be referred to as "Spiritual Bypass". To the best of my understanding this means to use "spiritual" concepts or philosophies to deny or escape "reality". There is no doubt that in the world of psychology this is an observable phenomenon. It can be quite common for people who are having difficulty coping with certain issues to seek an escape from them in spiritual communities and their teachings rather than acknowledge them or deal with them in the appropriate way.

But, to call this "Spiritual Bypass", is simply a by-product of a mind attempting to make sense of something that cannot be made sense of, and a complete lack of comprehension for what is being shared.

The mind has to conceptualise this into something that can be quantified, so that it can either be accepted as "true" or dismissed as "bullshit". The natural reality can never be realised by the mind as it is constantly replacing "what is" with what it thinks should or should not be. Either this *is* or *it isn't*, it cannot possibly be everything that *is and isn't*. Knowing is The Alpha and The Omega of all that appears for the mind, which is the mental expression of "me". It truly is easier for a camel to pass through the eye of a needle than it is for a rich man to enter heaven. Knowing is the currency for that which seeks.

If a friend were to confide that they were having difficulty coping with a serious issue, there is likely to be a natural concern and, if possible, an offering of support. Otherwise, it is highly probable that there would be a suggestion that they call someone or go to see someone who could help them in some way.

The body may become unwell. If so, there is likely to be an appropriate response. No doubt a visit to the doctor would happen. If the doctor prescribes medication, there may well be a taking of the medication, as would be the sensible thing to do. If there is poor health the response is likely to be appropriate to the problem, such as getting more exercise, or eating healthier foods and taking vitamins… *But no-one is doing that.*

There is no-one who has ever done anything…

There is no-one who ever could do anything…

Because, *there is no-one... ever!*

No-one has ever had a problem, no-one has ever helped anyone, no-one has ever tried to escape their reality, and no-one has ever gone to work, or driven a car, or visited Paris, or gotten sick, and there is certainly no-one who has ever tightrope walked across a canyon.

Just because there is an experience of a someone as doing these things, does not make it "real". Such is the nature of an illusion, *an experience that deceives by producing a false or misleading impression of reality**. In other words, "me", is a something that is perceived as being real, but, in the natural reality, is not.

* Ref: Cambridge English Dictionary

Everything is gently itself,

Just this nothing,

Arising from nowhere,

For no-one…

Innocence and Wonder

There is a kind of innocence in all of this. Almost like a remembering of something, or a time, so to speak, that was never actually forgotten. One could say there is the returning of a timeless child-like wonder that never actually left.

After the dissolving of the apparent "me" energy, there can be a period of exhaustion, for a short while. One could say that, metaphorically speaking, it is like getting home from a very, *very* long and stressful car journey, with an awkward and annoying passenger who never shuts up, and then silently sinking into a warm comfortable bed to sleep and recover… *Glorious!*

Then there can be more of a natural energy in the body, and in some ways a more simplistic, therefore, efficient functioning. That being said, there seems to be a great deal more sitting down happening here these days, and far less of an urgency to do anything. Yet, of course, doing still happens when necessary.

Being a "me" is an exhausting experience. It seems to take a huge amount of energy to maintain such a complicated, nuanced, illusory construct. It is as though the apparent separate energy *in* the body, leeches off the energy *of* the body. In that way, "me" is almost like a parasite that feeds on a natural energy, spontaneity, inspiration, creativity, and, one could say, sense of playfulness. Once there is nothing, there is suddenly *everything*.

The profound freedom in this aliveness is that nothing is taken so seriously anymore. Ultimately, the whole human drama is seen through, or seen as it is, which is only an appearance that is both "real" and "unreal".

Life becomes extremely simplistic and natural when it is no longer as experienced through the veil of a harder, wiser, knowing mind. In fact, it is no longer experienced at all. Everything that arises is always unknowing, immediate, and new, just like it is for the tiny child in timeless being. That is not to say that life stops appearing to throw the odd curve ball from time to time, but that is also the innocence and wonder of "this".

Dualism is that which observes, notices, or is aware of itself arising.

It is also that which is aware that it is aware of itself arising…

It is that which is aware of that which is aware of that which is aware of itself arising…

Ad infinitum…

Words on Thoughts

Of all that arises for "me" in the dream story, the most problematic seems to be the dealing with, or handling of, thoughts and emotions.

When I was a seeker, I tried for many years to practise ways to master, or at least gain some kind of control over my thoughts and thinking, but they always seemed to have their way with me in the end. I would mostly emerge from my time in contemplation feeling as though I had been mentally bombarded. So much so, that all contemplative practises began to be a thing of dread.

Meditation became more like an extreme sport than relaxing or enlightening. It could be relaxing or feel enlightening at times, but mostly, preparing to meditate was like preparing for a bungee jump. The sense of trepidation was often palpable as I was setting the timer before sitting to be alone with my thinking. If there was ever such a thing as The Thought Police, I would have been arrested and locked away long ago, never to be seen or heard of again!

Most spiritual teachings take the viewpoint that all suffering is thought created, or is a result of too much thinking, or the wrong kind of thinking. It is from this misunderstanding that many of the spiritual practises that we know and embrace, originate. They are aimed toward a controlling of thought, changing of thought, detaching from thought, transcending of thought, seeing through thought, or an embracing of thought. But thought, in and of itself, is entirely innocuous.

Thoughts and thinking are also just what's happening. They are like an internal intranet for the human being, an apparent energetic function that is informing and reporting, nothing more.

For the "person", thoughts and thinking are always being made into something personal. One could say that after the arising of self-awareness, this awareness now has an apparent separate position from which to begin to notice thoughts and thinking, and as with everything else that appears, it assumes ownership of thoughts and thinking by turning them into *my* thoughts and *my* thinking. Because thinking is now *my* thinking, it must have meaning and value, as it seems to be relevant to "me" and what is going on in "my life".

When there is no-one, thoughts are just no-thing "thought-ing". So, whatever comes up in the form of a thought is just that thought and does not necessarily mean anything or have to be applied to something. There is nothing left paying mind to thoughts or even listening to them anymore. The same is so for feelings and emotions. They are not personal; they just arise in a very natural way and then naturally pass, just like weather.

Of course, this is not "me's" experience. At any given time, there is a continual "checking in" going on with itself, *"How am I doing?"*, *"What's happening now?"*, *"How does this affect me?"*, and, *"What should I do about this?"*. This is why "me" loves therapy, because it gets to talk about all this stuff. Fundamentally, the problem for "me", is that it believes it is real, and therefore needs to work on having a better relationship with itself. When "me" dies, this is recognised, by no-one, as being just another absurd dynamic of the dualistic dream.

Some teachers of non-duality describe the arising of the "self" as an arising of a thought, and that separation is a misunderstanding which evolves out of this thought. "Self" is not an erroneous thought, idea, or false belief, it is purely energetic. It is a contracted sense of "here" which then gives rise to an experience of being separate from the whole. Along with the appearance of that illusory centre, come all kinds of thoughts, ideas, or beliefs about the nature of itself, all of which are an attempt to solidify and secure itself in the personal story. That's all "me" does.

Teachings of becoming are only of benefit in helping the seeker to have a better experience by making the prison of separation temporarily more bearable. The idea that the illusory "I" can become free by attempting to change the dynamic of the personal story only appears to happen within that particular story. Attempting to awaken oneself out of the dream is an utterly hopeless endeavour, because, intrinsically, an illusion cannot dispel itself.

All thoughts are "wholeness" arising as thought. So, in that sense liberation has nothing to do with a changing or dropping of certain thoughts, or a changing of beliefs, and it is certainly not a coming to know oneself as being beyond what is thought or believed. Every thought and every belief is already liberation. Even the thought or belief that "I am not free", is freedom appearing as that thought or belief.

As long as there is life as being experienced or observed, the freedom and aliveness that is "what is", is contained by the knowing of itself...

Words on Teachings

Everything is already itself. "This", is already the "absolute". Therefore, any attempt by the seeker to find that which is already, is like a wave trying to discover the ocean. Liberation is the absence of that which can become "liberated". There is nothing that needs to become, as there is already no-one. There is only the infinite ocean "wave-ing". So, there is nothing to be done, and no-one who can do it. Nothing needs to happen because it is already!

"What is", cannot be conceived of, realised, or understood, because there is no-one to realise or understand. How can something be learned, attained, or reached for when there is already everything? All that appears is already what is longed for, which is too wild and too free to be defined. Unknowing is unteachable because it is not knowable.

"This" cannot be pointed to because there are no separate positions to point from. Liberation eludes the seeker by also being seeking. It hides by already being everything. "This" is already home and seeking is perfectly "what is". Even those who teach non-duality from a dualistic understanding is liberation appearing as those teachers and their teachings.

There is no-one, and there is no separation. No-one is sitting in meditation, or observing awareness, or practising mindfulness, or trying to be more loving, compassionate, and altruistic, there is just what is apparently happening.

Spiritual experiences are just another appearance within the dreamed reality of "me", which is also just what is apparently happening. There can be no progression because nothing is actually moving. How could the "absolute everything" be something less or become something more? It is already the "absolute everything".

There is nothing that needs to be found for "this" to be "this". When self goes seeking for itself, or even for the absence of itself, it will only discover itself. That one can move oneself towards the divine, is the divine fallacy. The path of the seeker is like an infinite hallway made of mirrors, from which the "me" can never escape or see beyond. All it sees is itself. It is self-awareness reflecting the awareness of itself. Duality is the "knower" and the "seer", there are no mirrors, there is no awareness.

There is no duality. There is only the "absolute" being infinitely empty, which is also infinitely full. The absence of "I", is the absence of the reality in "reality". It is the end of the experience in "experience". It is the end of time in "time" and space in "space". It is the end of any and all notion that there is something else which lies dormant or unseen.
When the dream of "me" collapses, it is the end of all that believes itself to be, and therefore can become.

…Apparently…

A Little visit to the Cinema

There are teachers of "awakening" who describe the story of "me" as being like a movie projected onto a screen. Using this analogy, there is a pointing to an understanding or realization, which is that you are not the movie, you are the screen upon which the movie appears.

There is no you, and there is no story, therefore there are no distinctions to be made between a movie and a screen, even as a metaphor. That which creates such distinctions between an apparent movie and an apparent screen is the misunderstanding that there is a "you" who is having, or can have, an experience of being the movie and or the screen.

There is no movie and there is no screen. There is only what appears, which is unknowable. The story of "me" is an illusory experience of there being a "person" at the centre of whatever is appearing, who is real, autonomous, and has to look for something more meaningful as a way to add value to the experience of itself.

"Me" is the story, and the story is the "me", which is why the "me" cannot move itself out of the story by coming to have a deeper understanding of itself. The idea that "me" can change the story is just another story about "me" changing the story.

The story of "Me" is a constant seeking for meaning and purpose for that which experiences itself as not belonging and therefore must become.

A Glimpse in The Matrix

Sometimes there can be glimpses of "this". No-one has a glimpse. A glimpse is only recognised as being a glimpse with the returning of "me". Most often, it would seem, when people talk about having "glimpses", "awakenings", or a "seeing of non-duality", they are describing an experience of something as happening *to* them, not an absence of them. Such is the nature of all experience.

In this way, many descriptions of awakening, especially from those who claim to have "awakened", still sound as though they are coming from a dualistic understanding or mind. There seems to be an energy there that it is turning "this" into something that is or can be known. There is usually an ongoing story about a "someone" being or becoming a "no-one". Who can really say for sure if this is the case or not? And quite honestly, who cares! That's just what happens too.

Glimpses are a sudden disappearance of "me" into unknowing. It is not something that is or can be experienced. There were glimpses here, but it would have been impossible to tell someone what they were. There was absolutely no frame of reference to be able to even begin to describe what it was, let alone understand it. It was only when non-duality was heard being talked about in this rare and radical way, that the penny dropped, so to speak.

In the story of Neil Denham, there was a glimpse many years before it had ever occurred to me to start looking for something called "awakening". I had no idea what it was? But it was somehow never forgotten. The only reason it is mentioned is to highlight that glimpses have nothing to do with seeking, whatsoever. And the really bad news for the seeker is that they have nothing to do with apparent liberation either.

If a glimpse occurs for the seeker, once returned, the mind will usually begin to associate that glimpse with whatever seeking practise or activity they are involved with, so they will begin to do more of it or less of it, or whatever the case may be. The same is so for most "awakenings". When the appearance of "me" permanently disappears, it is just obvious that the end of "me" has no relevance at all to one's "spiritual condition", or to a so-called "seeing" of non-duality.

In some cases, glimpses can leave behind a certain flavour of the natural reality. After which, the seeker can be left with more of a hunger for liberation than ever. What is most disturbing, is that there can be a returning of the "me" energy, but now with a recognition, of sorts, of its own illusory-ness. This can bring with it a crippling realisation that there is nothing that "me" can do to bring about its own absence. In this way, glimpses can be more of a curse than a blessing because they are recognised as still happening in the dream story, and, therefore, can have no relevance to the end of the story.

For some, there can also be a lot of fear, or even terror, following a glimpse, as it is ultimately a glimpse of one's own death. But it is only a fear for the "me", of course.

I once read about the story of one man, who at a most desperate and crucial time in his life, had a sudden and profound awakening. He came back convinced that he had been touched by the very essence of God himself. And why not? It is as good an explanation as any, especially as this happened over eighty years ago, well before there were Yogis from India infiltrating Western culture with talks of oneness and the like.

He then started an entire culture based on this experience, which also involved the coming together of some other significant events. This became one of the biggest, and for its time, most innovative spiritual movements on the face of the planet to this day, and seems to have helped a lot of desperate people to have a better quality of life, (In the dream story, of course).

I later learned, that whilst attempting to write a second book expanding on the concepts of his spiritual program, he essentially had to be placed on full-time suicide watch because he was in so much personal anguish. At some point he had realised that his apparent awakening was no longer sustainable and felt himself to be more lost than ever.

This reportedly went on for nearly ten years. Ten years of crippling depression and self-loathing. You may or may not be glad to know that he pulled through and died naturally of old age in the end. From what I have read, he managed to arrive at a deep level of acceptance about all of this, which brought him some peace of mind before he died.

By all accounts this man had had an intimate and life changing awakening experience, but liberation did not appear.

What is longed for is already everywhere,

It is already "this", appearing as being hidden by the knowing of itself, and the looking for itself,

"This", is the "knower" and the "looker", which seeks to find itself,

Which is why itself is never found and the search is never ending,

...until the illusory seeker dies.

Words on Neurosis

I am approaching this tentatively, as one does not suddenly become an expert in neuroscience, quantum physics, cosmology, or any of that sort of stuff in liberation, despite what some teachers of "awakening" may attempt to convey in their books, seminars or lectures, *(Unless they are an "awakened" neuroscientist, quantum physicist, or cosmologist, of course!)*. So, this is more of a sense than anything else:

There still appears to be a certain neurochemistry that remains for a time after the "me" experience is over. There may even be some pathologies or behavioural patterns still running their course. There are bound to be certain neural pathways, or constructs in the brain, that have formed over a lifetime of its being subjected to, and conditioned by, the "me" story.

This is just an apparent human biology reacting and responding to what arises in the story. So, one would assume that these "energetic knots" will take some time to naturally unravel, or for those neurons to decay, once the story is over. There is a vast, *vast* difference between there being some residual neurosis and the frenetic neuroticism of the "me" energy. Without "me"*,* neurosis is no longer "me's" neurosis, it is just neurosis, and there is nothing that can or needs to be done with it because it is just another appearance.

When there is no longer an additional neurotic energy reacting and responding to it, any remaining neurosis is likely to get bored of showing up for a party when there is no-one to dance with anymore, and eventually stop bothering.

There is no suggestion here that one should or should not seek the appropriate help to process trauma or neurosis if it should arise. The suggestion is, that trauma or neurosis is also what arises for no-one.

Mind is the mental expression of "me", and only appears in the dream story.

There is no "me", and there is no "mind".

Words on Love

When I was on the spiritual path, I was ultimately looking for a deeper experience with love. I was looking for a connection with some kind of a loving energy that would flood into my life like an enriching, life-giving water, quenching the thirst for acceptance, drowning all fears, and turning the desert of existential loneliness into a garden of solitude.

Over the years I gave this energy many names and many faces in my attempts to conjure an appearance of the divine. I imagined that if this divine love could be found it would be the panacea for all my struggles, and I would live in a permanent state of blissful happiness. It is a fanciful dream, for sure, but that is all that it was.

For the "me", to seek love is to satisfy another longing or need. This longing is born out of the illusory experience of being a separate person who needs to find something in order to feel complete. It is the incessant longing for a return to being-ness, "this" being-ness which is boundless love, without limitation or conditionality.

"Me" wants to know a deeper love because in its separateness there is a fundamentally deep sense of insecurity. It constantly craves for an in-utero like state of comfort, warmth, and safety. To this end, there is a search for love, maybe in the romantic sense, or for the loving energy that is imagined will be experienced in spiritual awakening. But really, what it wants is for the search to be over. It assumes that the only way the search can end, is if the end is found.

Because "me" lives and moves in the story of itself, love will always come with certain conditions, or a list of requirements, in order to make it fit. For as long as there is the story, there will always be a role and a script for everyone and everything in the play of life. Love is at the heart of every story, but at the heart of *the* story there is only "me". Even if the ideal love is found, in the ideal way, with the ideal someone, or in the ideal something, for the seeker, there is still a feeling of incompleteness, so there will still be seeking.

There are world renowned religious and spiritual leaders who tell us that the way to enlightenment is through something called unconditional love. They give instruction or advice on how to move towards this realisation of love through practise and cultivation, self-sacrifice, and charity. They maintain that the keeping of certain conditions can somehow be used to discover that which is unconditional and "unconditionable".

This is all quite innocent of course, it comes out of a misunderstanding that was passed to them, so they pass it on to others, and so on, and so on. Unconditional love is unquestionably the original essence of religion, it has just become lost through centuries of miscomprehension, manipulation, and dogma.

In liberation there is a profound falling in love with everything, but it is not for anyone or any thing. One could almost say that it is the falling in love with life itself, but there is no-one left to do this, and no-one has a life to fall in love with anymore. Unconditional love only becomes obvious with the end of the story, in which the appearance of "me" dies. Death is the end of the story, whether it be with the death of the body or in liberation.

Unconditional love is not a something to be discovered by the planting of a seed that can be cultivated and grown. It cannot be created, invited, moved into, or held on to, because unconditional love *is already what's happening*. In this way, liberation is the absolute unconditional falling in love, that never actually happens.

There is nothing that can be said about unconditional love without containing it. There are no words that can describe it without labelling it. Words are, by their very design, descriptive. They are used in the describing of something that is known, or so that something can be known. This love cannot be known. There is still an ocean of "indescribableness" between what can be said, what is said, and "what is".

This is not the kind of love that the seeker can imagine, and this is not the kind of love that the seeker is looking for, as this is not a love that the seeker can have. It lies beyond all understanding and all ownership. It is a being cut loose from all apparent ties and all apparent relationship. When there is nothing left to fall in love, or fall in love with anymore, there is only love. So, in that sense, it is an overwhelming abundance, which is also absolute poverty.

This love is all embracing, yet it embraces nothing. It is all encompassing, but its circumference is nowhere. It is joy, and it is sadness. It is peace beyond imagining, and it is violence, ferocity, and chaos. It is to live in perfect harmony, and it is a nuclear bomb. It is gut wrenching fear, cruelty, pain, and suffering, and it is patting a dog, playing with a child, drinking tea, or making love. It is a falling into boundlessness, infinite and free, and it is the appearance of not being free.

There was a sadness and sense of loss that arose here recently with the death of a friend. He was in so much psychological distress that he suicided. That sadness is unconditional love being sadness. The death of a friend is unconditional love appearing as death and the sense of loss. It is loss as being impersonal; therefore, it is whole and complete in its "loss-ness".

When there is no-one, there is no need for there to be a letting go or embracing of sadness, it is just sadness. Equally, there is no-one that needs to hold on to happiness, joy, wonder, or even a sense of "in love-ness". This is love without conditions, without limitations, and without the need to be anything other than what's happening.

That which never began, is already over…

The Glass is Always Empty

"This", is so obvious that it is always overlooked in the looking for it,
It cannot to be found as it is already everywhere, and it is nowhere,

"There", any empty glass,
For the individual it is just a glass,
Another object arising within the subjective experience,
In this way the glass is all that is known,
It is dead, boring, and assumed...

In the dreamt reality, a simple glass cannot possibly be the aliveness that is sought, because it is just a glass,
In the natural reality, the glass is constantly singing with aliveness,
It is the aliveness of "what is" and the wonder of what isn't...

In dying the glass is no longer a glass at all,
It is unconditional love,
It is the great mystery somehow appearing to be a glass,
It is vibrantly alive and free because of the unknowingness of it all...

"What is", is deafening,
An energetic cacophony of chaos which appears as being ever so gently and tenuously ordered,
... As though the appearance itself could fall away into the no-thingness that it is, without a whisper of its ever having been,
This tender delicacy is lost within the "here-ness" and "there-ness" of knowing...

*The appearance of a simple glass, just as it is, is continually
calling us back to that which is always home,
"This" home that was never left...*

*This is so, so, simple, that the individual, with all its vagaries
and complexities couldn't possibly see the everyday ordinary
as the natural marvel of being...*

*Yet, there it is... No-thing "glass-ing",
Singing the song of the formless forming,
Unassuming and absolutely whole.*

All forms of self-enquiry are a self-confirmatory experience, and serve only to support the illusory construct of the individual,

A questioned self is still itself,

Who would be questioning into who?

Smoke and Mirrors

Non-duality is unknowable.

Knowing is the dream.

To know a knowing, is a dream within the dream.

There are dreams within dreams within dreams, which is the dream appearing as so.

There cannot be a pointing to the dream from within the dream.

From within the dream, the dream is all that is seen.

The end of the dream is the end of the one who is seeing.

That there is one who can awaken from the dream, is a dream from which one cannot awaken.

No-one awakens because there is no-one dreaming.

There is no awareness as there is no-one who is aware.

There is no awareness that is aware of itself as awareness.

Without a something for awareness to be aware of, it ceases to be aware.

There is no consciousness seeking to have an experience of itself as consciousness, because everything is unknowing.

There is no inner and outer, or worlds within worlds, because there is nothing that is separate from the whole, which includes an appearance of separation.

There is no perception of oneness, as there are no positions from which oneness can be perceived.

There is no oneness.

There is only this "aliveness" appearing to happen without a centre that witnesses or observes.

"This" is always immediate and whole, as being beyond the conceptual, and beyond all understanding.

There is no "non-duality" because this is always "not two".

Nothing does not become everything, and everything cannot become nothing,

Nothing is everything, and everything is nothing,

Therefore, "this" is never lost or lacking.

Resonance and Resonating

If there is a resonance with what is being shared here, or in a radical non-duality meeting, it is not the seeker who resonates.

No-one resonates with this message.

There is no resonance happening "here", or happening "there", there is only resonance happening, or not, which is the "absolute everything" resonating, or not.

If there is a sense of "home", it is not sensed by that which experiences itself as being lost. It is "home" appearing as a sense of itself.

"This" is home.

No-one ever left.

Energy abhors a vacuum; Even emptiness is full.

Timelessness

We are all born into timelessness, and timeless being is all there is.

"This" is not actually moving.

"This" has not come from anywhere, and it is not going anywhere.

There is an appearance of movement, but it is stillness appearing to move, and all movement appears to be still.

Past and future are "this" appearing as a memory of the past and an assumption of a future. There is no "real" past or future, there is only what appears.

That is as close as I can get to describing Timelessness.

Who would be killing a Buddha on the side of the road?

I Dream of Buddha

There are certain words which seem to paint more of an elaborate picture in the mind than others.

"Enlightenment" is certainly one of those words and will always come with a huge amount of baggage attached to it, which is far from the apparent reality of liberation.

"Enlightenment" seems to conjure up an image like one of those murals you see painted onto the wall of a temple of Buddha or Krishna and his enlightened followers.

It is usually full of golden lotus flowers, bizarre looking creatures, men with "blissed out" facial expressions and shimmering auras, and then there is always the dancing women and children who have become so ecstatic in their rapture, it appears to have turned them blue.

The word or term, "enlightenment", has no significance of any kind because it has no reality at all. It's a fairy tale. One would do just as well to have a mural of Disney films and their characters painted onto a wall in a school classroom.

When the one melts into the whole, so do the many,

When the subject disappears, so do all objects,

When "two" appears as "not two", the "one" was never here,

So, there is nothing left that needs to become.

The Lake of Nirvana

There was once an enlightened Master who claimed to have been to what he called the "The Lake of Nirvana". He had apparently done so through many years study of the way of the Samurai and the secret teachings of an ancient Japanese Zen school. He was in many ways a remarkable and impressive man, who seemed to have surmounted or surpassed all obstacles in his path, through focus, discipline, and mastery of the self.

His whole deportment was that of a man with the answer. Indeed, he claimed to have committed "spiritual seppuku" and been energetically reborn into his former Master's robes. Therefore, the duty now fell to him to take the students to The Lake of Nirvana. The only requirement was that they bow to him and were devoted to his Master's school.

Beneath the teachings of wisdom, love, and peace, was an atmosphere of aggression, intimidation, and even threats of violence towards any who questioned the will and wisdom of the Master. There were brothers who rejected and shamed their brothers in order to curry their Master's favour. People were abused and relationships were ruined through subtle manipulations, coercion, and control… All because there was a promise of the lake.

The lake was not available to all, only to those who could actively demonstrate their loyalty and devotion, again and again and again. Only one who could prove themselves as being worthy of such a gift was invited to join the Master on the shore.

Only those who acquiesced and could manage to dig a little deeper into their own pockets or the pockets of their families, were able to come home. Only those who were willing to surrender everything to one man and his borrowed wisdom were on their way to the way.

There were some who truly believed themselves as being on the way to the way. They had done everything right and seemed to have been thus far rewarded for their sure footedness. But then the lake appeared to move, and the way would inevitably change.

What was sought, now lay hidden at the top of the next mountain… and then the next… and then the next. But that did not matter, they trusted their Master and had already come so far. There had been too much invested, so there was now too much at stake, to risk losing sight of the increasingly elusive lake.

I wonder if there is still a Master making promises, delivering sermons, and offering that which cannot be given, by pointing to that which cannot be found?

I wonder if there are still those who follow a man who promises to them the air they already breath, in return for more of the blood they are already bleeding?

I wonder how many still dream of mountains and lakes, contented that they are on their way, or devastated that they were undeserved of that which is always available?

There is no way…

Death is not the end of a life; it is the end of a birth,

There is no "real" death, as nothing really lives,

Everything is just what appears as coming into being,

Which is simply "this", as it is and isn't,

"This" is already death as being infinitely alive and infinitely free.

Nothing Happening

This simply arises out of nothing, so in that sense, there isn't a "message". There is no need for anything to be expressed or communicated. There is no agenda to satisfy or intention to be helpful. There is no-one to be helpful and there is no-one to help. When it is recognised that there isn't and never was a "me", "me" is no longer recognised in others. When I died, so did you.

One could say that this is a responding to an energy, which is boundless energy responding to an apparent trapped energy. This is freedom responding to something that experiences itself as not being free. So, there can be a writing about this, or a talking about this, but it will never bring one closer to or further from "this", because "this" is already that freedom.

What is shared here is not exclusive, nor does it have to be inclusive. This is entirely free to be whatever it is, however it arises, as whatever is being said. But mostly, this is about what is not, or cannot be said. "Boundlessness" cannot be translated into words. Although words are energy and some seem to have an energy of their own, this is a communication beyond all verbal communication.

Everything is energy appearing to react and respond to energy. There is no creator, source, or origin from which everything appears because everything is nothing. "What is", is never coming into existence or winking out of existence. "This" has not come from anywhere and it is not going anywhere.

There are no beginnings, endings, or eternities. Time, in whatever form, is experiential as relative to space. When the experiential is no more, there is no more experience of time and space as being relative to anything fixed or real. There is only timeless spaceless-ness, "is-ing" and "isn't-ing".

There is no journey or arrival at a destination. There isn't a "coming home" or a "returning to being-ness", because "this" is already home, and being-ness is all there is. This is the paradox of liberation, nothing is ever seen or understood. There is a total collapse of that which needs to see or understand, without ever seeing or understanding. Nothing is reached or attained, the need for attainment simply dies, and liberation appears.

There is no suggestion that it is better or worse for there to be a "me" or no "me", or that there should not be an experience of separation. This is not a denial of that appearance. The dream of "I am" is the "absolute" appearing as that dream, but from within the dream, the dream is absolute. This is an exposing of that illusion as it appears. There is no need for there to be an awakening from the dream, as it has no reality at all. There are no awakenings.

This really is, as far as it can be, all about "nothing". This is "nothing" writing. Words and sentences are "nothing" happening. This is "nothing" being rain falling, wind blowing, trees moving, the sound of passing cars in the street, and a bird singing just outside the window. All of it without need or purpose, or the need for purpose. "This" is no more significant than a leaf dropping from a branch. It is just what appears.

There is no meaning of life or meaning to life. That is its freedom. Life does not need a reason to be alive. There is already aliveness everywhere, which is everything being unconditionably alive and free.

There is nothing trapped. There is nothing that needs to collapse or fall away. There is nothing that is not already liberation. "This", is "nothing" appearing as liberation or being liberated. There is no liberation.

There is no great revelation. Revelations are only revelations in their revealing. Once revealed, they are just what is obviously already "what is". Nothing is revealed, as there is nothing being obscured.

Everything that appears is "nothing" simply appearing. This is "nothing" appearing as every thought, feeling or emotion. Every taste, touch, sound, smell, or sight is this "nothing", which is why everything that appears is both "real" and "unreal".

Unknowing permeates everything and is everything. This is utterly inexpressible because it is totally unknowable. It is not even a thing. It is everywhere and nowhere. Empty and full.

"This" will always remain forever illusive, unfathomable, indistinguishable, unspeakable, and uncommunicable…
… *but is always wonderfully… stunningly… and heart achingly perfect.*

There is an Epilogue (But it isn't Special)

There really isn't anything special about liberation or the "seeing" of "this". There is nothing special about this author, or in what the author is attempting to describe.

Of course, the seeker cannot help but turn this communication into something seen or imagined as being in some way special, but if the seeker knew what is really being described, it would be extremely disappointed. Fortunately for the seeker, it never gets to see the natural reality because it cannot survive liberation.

This is, however, what is truly being longed for, which is an end to seeking. Not because seeking comes to an end, there is merely a recognition that there is no-one seeking. It is a profound recognition, to be sure, but it is not the great spiritual climax that the seeker expects. This message is about something amazingly simple and ordinary.

In many ways, you could say liberation is the most profound inconvenience, *especially if you still have plans!* It is the end of "you", and it is the end of "your life". "You" doesn't actually want liberation. Not that there is a say in it, of course, either your head is in the tiger's mouth or it is not, and who knows what the tiger will do?

As this is being written, I am sitting in the old Victorian garden outside my home. There is no mystical experience happening, no awareness, no radiating auras, or earth vibrations, no music of the spheres, no spirit dancing in the treetops.

There is, however, a vibrancy, an aliveness, and a gentle sweetness to everything and in everything, all of which, is simply the great mystery appearing...

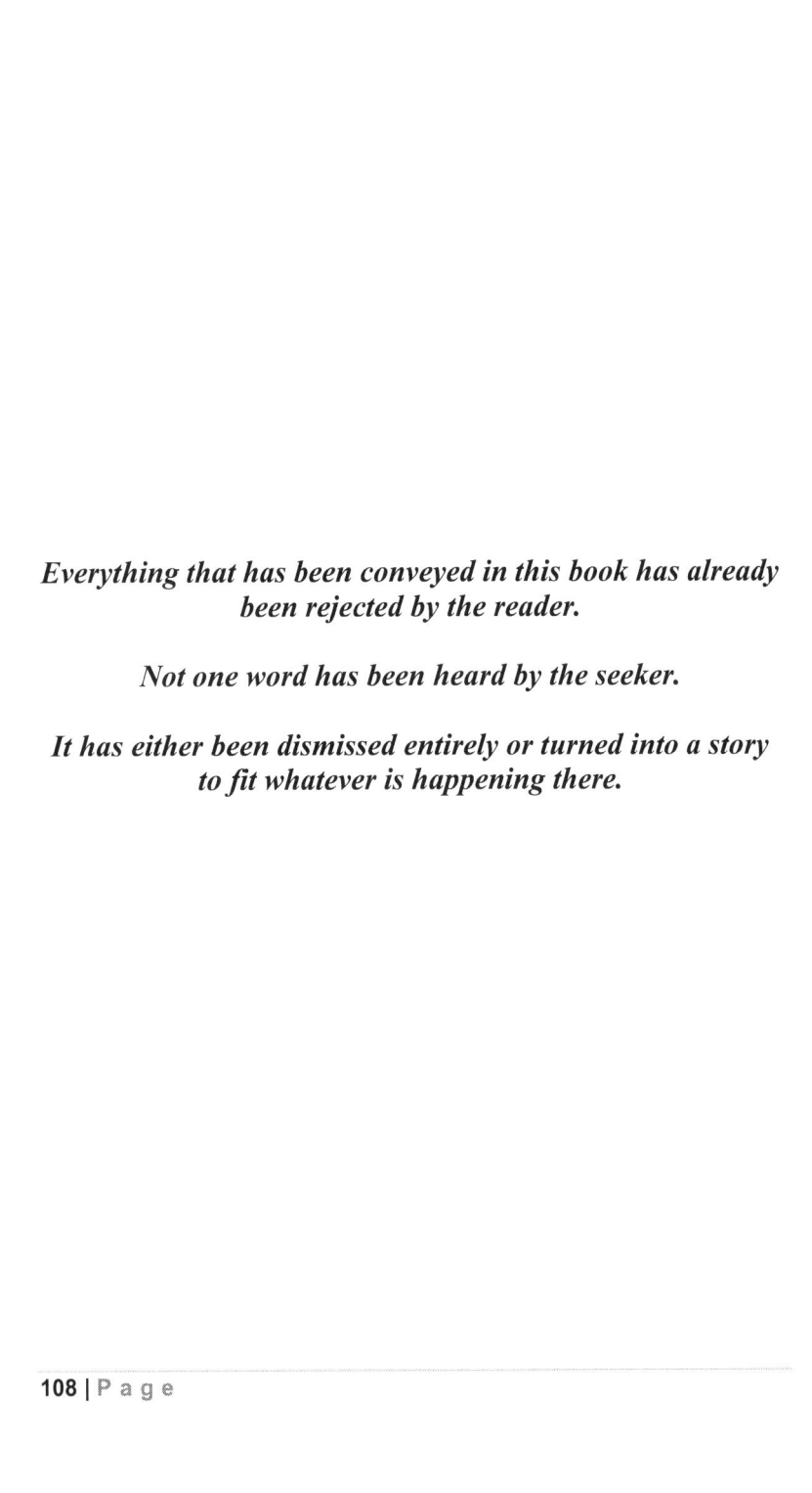

Everything that has been conveyed in this book has already been rejected by the reader.

Not one word has been heard by the seeker.

It has either been dismissed entirely or turned into a story to fit whatever is happening there.

If you would like to contact Neil, you can do so by email at

neildenham2015@gmail.com

Thank You

Printed in Great Britain
by Amazon